ANCIENT GREECE

Written by
Steve and Patricia Harrison

Illustrated by
Wayne Anderson, David Ashby, Philip Hood, Brent Linley
and Shirley Mallinson

Edited by
Caroline White

Designed by
Peter Shirtcliffe

Picture research by
Helen Taylor

CONTENTS

The march of time

6000BC — 2000BC

Stone Age statue of mother goddess

Minoan civilisation on Crete

1100BC — 1000BC

Dorian Greeks invade the mainland

Ionian Greeks found colonies

750BC — 650BC — 480BC

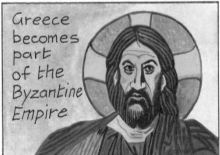

Greek alphabet created

```
EV⊕EPONACOCON
MꝆO7ΔO?)VPꝜKꓤΔꝜ
EMΔFSKꓱTATⵁPV
MVꝜꓕAWΛVꓤEWꝜ
WASTVPAΔSKAΔEN7
```

Tyrants begin to take power

Battle of Salamis

AD395 — AD1460

Greece becomes part of the Byzantine Empire

Greece becomes part of the Ottoman Empire

..00 BC · 1250 BC

haft raves t Iycenae

Trojan War

..0 BC · 776 BC

our illages oin ogether o form parta

The first Olympic Games

334 BC · 30 BC

Alexander the Great invades Asia

Romans control Hellenic world

1829 · AD 1967 · AD 1975

reece becomes independent

Dictatorship of generals

Democracy returns to Greece

Legacy of the Ancient Greeks

The way we live today has been influenced by people who lived at other times and in other places. The words we use, the food we eat, the books we read, the games we play, our buildings and much much more are part of the legacy of the past.

One of the most important legacies is that of Ancient Greece. Here are just a few examples of how the Ancient Greeks have influenced our world today.

Atoms

A Greek philosopher called Democritus (460–370 BC) claimed that everything was made up of small particles.

The Olympics

The first Olympic Games were held in 776 BC at the Greek city of Olympia.

Theatre

The word 'theatre' is Greek. Most modern theatres follow the Greek plan.

The Bible

The New Testament was first written in Greek. The word 'bible' comes from the Greek word *biblia*, which means 'books'.

Marathon

Pheidippides ran from Athens to Sparta to ask for help against the Persians just before the Battle of Marathon (490 BC). The distance of a marathon today is 42 195 metres.

Alphabet

The Ancient Greeks played an important part in the development of the alphabet. The first two letters of the Greek alphabet – alpha and beta – have given us the word 'alphabet'.

Architecture

Throughout the world, buildings have been constructed in the styles of Ancient Greece. The British Museum in London is an example of this.

Democracy

The word 'democracy' is Greek. It means 'government by the people'.

Words

Many words that we use today were first used in Ancient Greece. Others have been made by joining together Greek words.

Word used today	Greek origin of word
orchestra	*orkheisthai* = to dance
biology *(bio-logy)*	*bios* = life *logos* = word
geology *(geo-logy)*	*ge* = earth *logos* = word
geography *(geo-graphy)*	*ge* = earth *graphia* = writing

Ancient and modern Greece

Ancient Greece was not a single country under one ruler. It was made up of small groups of people with local rulers and governments. Many of the Greek communities had their own dialect, currency and rules for living.

Greece today

Capital city: Athens

Currency: Drachma

Population: 10 047 000

GAUL

IBERIA

Marseille

Nice

CORSICA

Alalia

ITALY

Tarraco

Cumae
Naples
Posidonia

Saguntum

Tharrus

Ele

SARDINIA

MEDITERRANEAN
SEA

Rhegiu

Himera   Messar

SICILY

Utica

Agrigentum

Megara Hyblaea

Carthage

Syracuse

NUMIDIA

Leptis Mag

Sometimes the different groups fought against each other. Gradually the Greeks came to share a common language and the same religious beliefs, but they were not citizens of a single country.

The map on these two pages shows the world of the Ancient Greeks. In some areas most of the population was Greek, while in others a city was built by Greek settlers but was surrounded by people who had very different ways of living.

The border of modern Greece is shown on the map by the blue line.

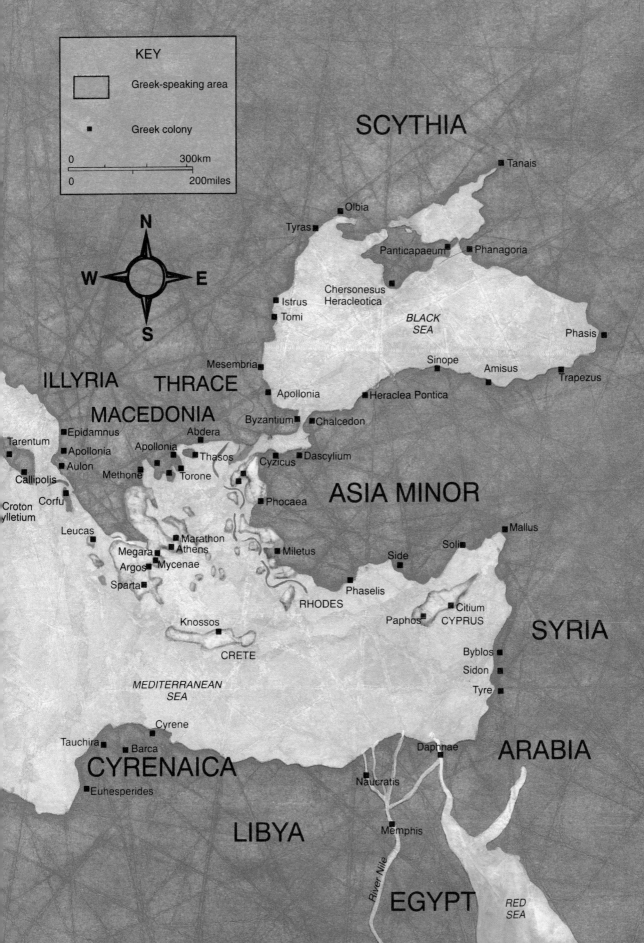

KEY

Greek-speaking area

■ Greek colony

0   300km

0   200miles

N
W   E
S

SCYTHIA

■ Tanais

■ Olbia

Tyras ■

Panticapaeum ■   ■ Phanagoria

■ Istrus
■ Tomi

Chersonesus
Heracleotica

*BLACK
SEA*

■ Phasis

■ Sinope
   ■ Amisus
■ Trapezus

Mesembria ■

ILLYRIA   THRACE

■ Apollonia

■ Heraclea Pontica

MACEDONIA

Byzantium ■ ■ Chalcedon

■ Epidamnus   ■ Abdera

Tarentum

■ Apollonia Apollonia ■

■ Aulon   ■ Thasos

Callipolis Methone ■ ■ Torone

■ Cyzicus ■ Dascylium

Croton
ylletium Corfu ■

■ Phocaea

ASIA MINOR

■ Leucas

■ Marathon
■ Athens

■ Miletus

Megara ■   ■
Argos ■ ■ Mycenae

Sparta ■

■ Side

■ Soli

■ Mallus

Phaselis ■

RHODES

Citium ■
Paphos ■ CYPRUS

SYRIA

■ Knossos

CRETE

Byblos ■

Sidon ■

Tyre ■

*MEDITERRANEAN
SEA*

Cyrene ■

Tauchira ■ ■ Barca

Daphnae ■

ARABIA

CYRENAICA

■ Euhesperides

Naucratis ■

LIBYA

Memphis ■

River Nile

EGYPT *RED
SEA*

Theseus and the Minotaur

GREEK LEGEND TELLS OF A POWERFUL KING OF CRETE CALLED MINOS. PEOPLE THOUGHT HE WAS JUST AND FAIR.

I WILL NEVER FORGIVE THE ATHENIANS FOR KILLING ANDROGEUS. THEY WILL PAY AGAIN THIS YEAR — I WILL FEED THE MINOTAUR WITH THEIR HUMAN FLESH.

HOWEVER, HE WAS ANGRY AT THE DEATH OF HIS SON.

KING MINOS KEPT A HIDEOUS MONSTER, THE MINOTAUR, WHICH WAS HALF BULL AND HALF MAN. IT LIVED IN AN ENORMOUS MAZE UNDER THE PALACE AT KNOSSOS.

EVERY YEAR THE PEOPLE OF ATHENS SENT SEVEN YOUNG WOMEN AND SEVEN YOUNG MEN TO THE ISLAND OF CRETE TO BE FED TO THE MINOTAUR.

AEGEUS, KING OF ATHENS, FELT HELPLESS.

THESEUS, I AM WEAK. IF I REFUSE TO SEND THEM, MINOS WILL ATTACK US WITH HIS GREAT ARMY AND MANY MORE THAN FOURTEEN LIVES WILL BE LOST.

FATHER, I CANNOT STAND BY AND WATCH THIS HAPPEN. I MUST GO AND KILL THIS EVIL WHICH HANGS OVER OUR CITY YEAR AFTER YEAR.

If Theseus succeeded in killing the Minotaur, he was to change the ship's black sails to white on his return. Aegeus would wait on the cliffs and pray that he would see white sails and know his son was safe.

The fourteen young Athenians, including Theseus, arrived at Knossos and awaited their fate.

During the night, Princess Ariadne, King Minos' daughter, secretly entered Theseus' cell.

If you will take me back to Athens as your wife, I will show you a way out of the maze.

Theseus agreed.

Ariadne had given Theseus a ball of string to help him retrace his steps. He tied one end to a rock and let the string slowly unwind as he felt his way through the dark passages.

The Athenians were to be thrown to their death one at a time. If they were not eaten by the Minotaur, they would never find their way out of the maze and would starve to death. Theseus was the first to enter.

The snore of the Minotaur became louder and louder. Then at last he saw the creature asleep on the floor.

Theseus dragged the monster to its feet, and, though it fought wildly, he killed it with his bare hands.

Ariadne had planned the escape well. As their ship sailed away, they felt the island shake. It was an earthquake. They watched the great palace of Knossos crumble and burn. That was the end of Crete's power.

Aegeus stood on the cliffs awaiting the ship's return.

The ship appeared on the horizon. But its sails were black. Aegeus thought his son must be dead and threw himself off the cliff. Theseus, in his excitement, had forgotten to change the sails.

Crete: Minoan civilisation

Crete is a large island south of the Greek mainland. A great civilisation developed there between 2200 and 1400 BC. This civilisation has been given the name 'Minoan', after the legendary King Minos.

The people of Crete at that time did not speak Greek. They are important in the history of Ancient Greece because the Greeks who later conquered the island learnt from them. The culture of Crete became part of the civilisation of Ancient Greece.

Crete was a fertile island. Food and wine were produced in large amounts. Because of its position, trade also developed. Merchants traded with Egypt, Syria and the cities to the north.

The palace at Knossos

The rulers of the time built magnificent palaces. The first was at Knossos. There were no large walls for defence, so it seems that Minoan civilisation was peaceful. The palace was also very luxurious. The queen's chamber had running water and a flush-type toilet. Superb pottery, jewellery and small figures have also been found at Knossos.

The fashions, sports, religious beliefs and pastimes of the nobles were painted on the walls of the palace. The fresco on page 11 shows three acrobats leaping over a bull.

Storage jars from the palace at Knossos for holding oil and wine

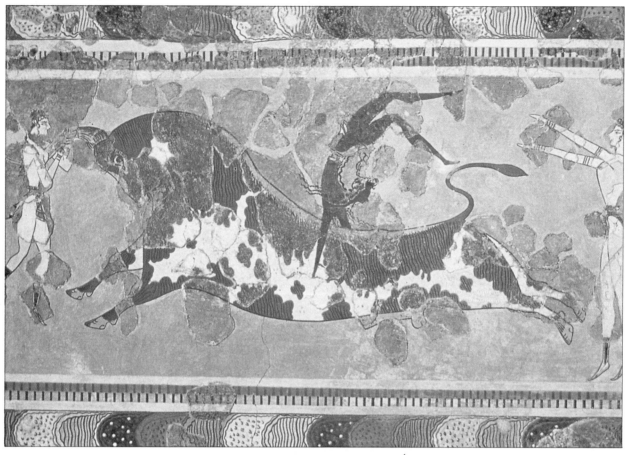

The spectacular and dangerous sport of bull-leaping is shown on this fresco from Knossos.

The story of Theseus and the Minotaur is a Greek myth. As in many stories, some parts are based on events which really happened. The work of archaeologists can help sort myth from reality.

In 1894 the archaeologist Arthur Evans went to Crete and bought the land on which the palace had once stood. He uncovered a civilisation that was four thousand years old. The ruins of the palace were spread over 2 hectares of land. There were signs that it had beer destroyed by an earthquake and fire.

While there was no evidence of a maze, the palace itself was like a maze with hundreds of rooms.

Arthur Evans used archaeological evidence to rebuild parts of the palace. Some people said it looked like a Victorian hotel when he had finished.

■ Go back to the story of Theseus and the Minotaur and list the parts which you think are based on fact.

■ Why do you think some people criticised Arthur Evans for rebuilding the palace?

Mycenae

A new civilisation began to develop on
mainland Greece around 1600 BC.
Warlike rulers built palaces with high
defensive walls on hilltops from
where they could control the
local countryside.
The finest of these
palaces was at
Mycenae.

Mycenae was not a capital city. It was just one of many powerful cities. We call this part of Greek history the period of Mycenaean civilisation (1600–1100 BC).

Mycenaeans crossed the sea and conquered other cities and islands, including the Minoan civilisation of Crete. As the Mycenaeans travelled, they spread the Greek language and took objects and ideas from the people they conquered.

Plan of Ancient Mycenae

Archaeologists record the exact position of
everything they find beneath the earth.
Plans of a whole site are then drawn.
These help us to understand the past.

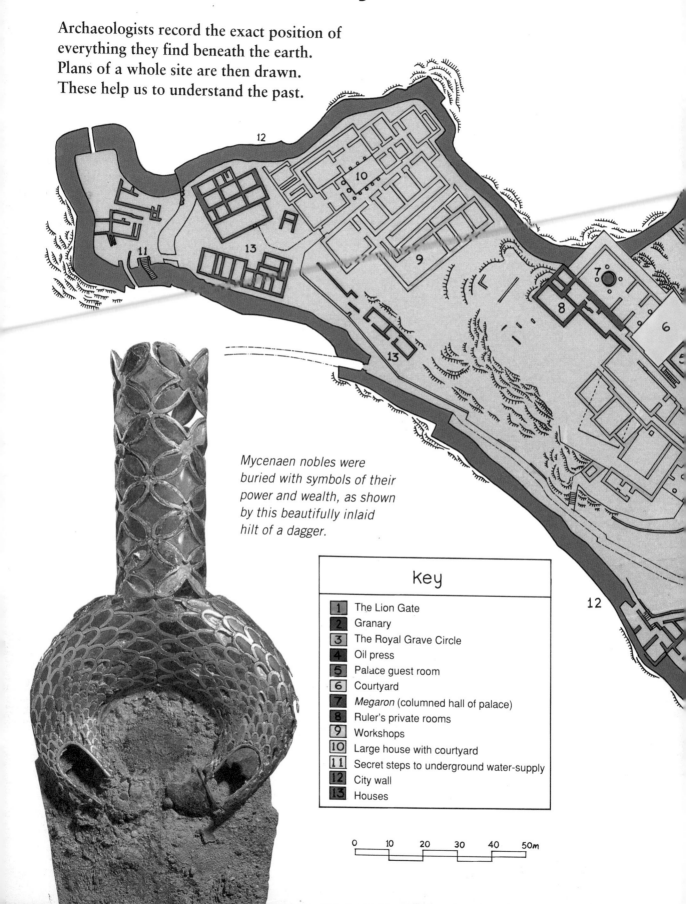

*Mycenaen nobles were
buried with symbols of their
power and wealth, as shown
by this beautifully inlaid
hilt of a dagger.*

Key

1	The Lion Gate
2	Granary
3	The Royal Grave Circle
4	Oil press
5	Palace guest room
6	Courtyard
7	*Megaron* (columned hall of palace)
8	Ruler's private rooms
9	Workshops
10	Large house with courtyard
11	Secret steps to underground water-supply
12	City wall
13	Houses

0   10   20   30   40   50m

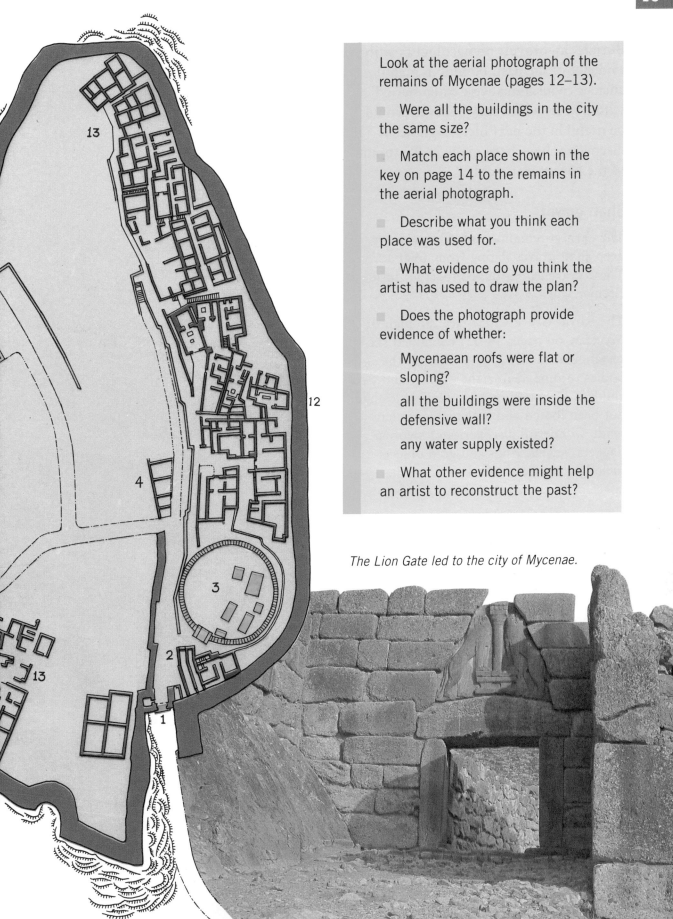

Look at the aerial photograph of the remains of Mycenae (pages 12–13).

■ Were all the buildings in the city the same size?

■ Match each place shown in the key on page 14 to the remains in the aerial photograph.

■ Describe what you think each place was used for.

■ What evidence do you think the artist has used to draw the plan?

■ Does the photograph provide evidence of whether:

Mycenaean roofs were flat or sloping?

all the buildings were inside the defensive wall?

any water supply existed?

■ What other evidence might help an artist to reconstruct the past?

The Lion Gate led to the city of Mycenae.

Royal burials

Burials can provide archaeologists with evidence of the past. Nobles in many ancient civilisations were often buried with objects which they believed would be useful in the next life. Magnificent discoveries have been made in the tombs of the Mycenaean nobles.

Shaft graves

The earliest remains from Mycenae are deep shaft graves dating from 1600 BC. These graves are grouped together inside circular walls.

The Royal Grave Circle (see the plan of Mycenae on pages 14–15) contained six rectangular family graves. In total the bodies of nine men, eight women and two children have been found. The graves had not been looted and archaeologists have made wonderful discoveries of swords, daggers, jewels, rings and gold objects, including the death mask seen on the cover of this book and the crown below.

Above each grave stood a stone *stele* (gravestone). The evidence from these shows that the people buried at Mycenae were warriors and hunters.

The most recent discovery of a grave circle at Mycenae was in 1951. Perhaps there are still more waiting to be discovered.

After completion the shaft was filled with earth

carved gravestone

Shaft grave

Gold crown found in a Mycenaean shaft grave

Tholos tomb

Entrance to a tholos tomb

Treasury of Atreus		
Entrance path (dromos)	36 metres long	
	6 metres wide	
Doorway (stomion)	5.4 metres high	
	2.66 metres wide	
Inside	14.5 metres in diameter	
	13.2 metres high	

Tholos tombs

About 1500 BC, the rulers of the Mycenae area changed and a new burial custom was introduced. Large beehive-shaped tombs were built of stone. They are known as *tholos* tombs. The bodies of family members were placed on the ground alongside each other.

Nine *tholos* tombs have been discovered at Mycenae. Seven are in the hills away from the city wall. The most impressive is known as the Treasury of Atreus, although it was not a treasury.

The great city wall and the palace at Mycenae were built after 1250 BC, later than most of the *tholos* tombs.

The story of Schliemann

Tales of Greek heroes, some from the time of the Mycenaeans, were passed down over the centuries. A Greek poet called Homer is believed to have used these stories as the basis for two long poems. The first poem is called the *Iliad* and the second is the *Odyssey*. The *Iliad* dates from about 700 BC. It tells the story of the Greek war against the Trojans and the siege of the city of Troy.

In the nineteenth century many people believed that Homer's stories were just fairy tales, legends of long ago that were not based on real places or real people. Some writers said Troy had never existed. They believed Homer had simply made it up. But one man was certain that Troy did exist, and he set out to find it. That man was Heinrich Schliemann.

When I am big, I shall go myself to find Troy and the king's treasure.

In 1829, when he was seven years old, Heinrich was given a picture book in which there was an artist's drawing of the city of Troy.

His father told him that nothing was left of Troy. No one even knew where it stood.

When Heinrich grew up, he worked all over the world as a merchant. He learned many languages and his businesses were successful.

You're wasting your time.

Then one day, having become rich and famous, he decided to leave his work and set out in search of the remains of Troy.

Heinrich believed that what he read in the *Iliad* was true, and that it would help him find the city of Troy. Others laughed.

Heinrich visited Burnabashi, which others said was the site of Troy. But when he compared the place with Homer's writing, he decided that it could not possibly be the right site. So he moved to Hissarlik, where he decided to dig.

Heinrich discovered not one Troy but the ruins of nine cities. Each city had been built on the ruins of the previous one. When he discovered treasure, he thought it dated from the time of Homer. In fact it was from even earlier in history.

The sixth city of Troy is thought to have looked like this.

What the *Iliad* says	The evidence at Hissarlik
The Greeks travelled from their boats to Troy several times a day.	The site was one hour from the coast.
The city was surrounded by a wall and contained a great palace.	There was a large, flat, raised mound of land.
Achilles and Hector ran three full circles round Troy during their fight.	The land sloped gently around the city. There were no steep sides.

The city-states

The Ancient Greeks did not think of themselves as a single nation. They lived in small scattered settlements throughout mainland Greece, the islands, Asia Minor and Italy. Each settlement thought of itself as an independent city-state.

A city-state was called a *polis*. Most had a government, a large open space known as the *agora* for markets and public meetings, courts, a defensive wall and farmland around the city. Each city-state was ruled in different ways at different times.

Temple

Agora

What the Greeks in the city-states had in common

Greek language (*spoken in dialects*)	The earliest writings that have been found are from the eighth century BC.
gods	The same gods were worshipped across all the city-states.
oracle at Delphi	The Greeks were guided by the advice which the oracle gave about the future.
Olympia and its games	All the city-states gathered every four years in Olympia for the games.
legends of the past	The Greeks shared legends found in the *Iliad* and the *Odyssey*.
Greek heroes	All Greeks could admire the actions of heroes such as Heracles (better known to us under his Roman name of Hercules).

Aristocratic government

About 700 BC, most Greek city-states were ruled by a king (*basileus*) who came from the local nobles. The nobles played a part in government. Sparta was different and had two kings.

Tyrannical government

In most city-states between 650 and 500 BC, tyrants took power by leading revolts against the nobles. Many cities had fine buildings erected by the tyrants.

Democratic government

Some Greek city-states removed the tyrants. Rule was by citizens of the state. The people (*demos*) made the laws. The word 'democracy' means 'government by the people'.

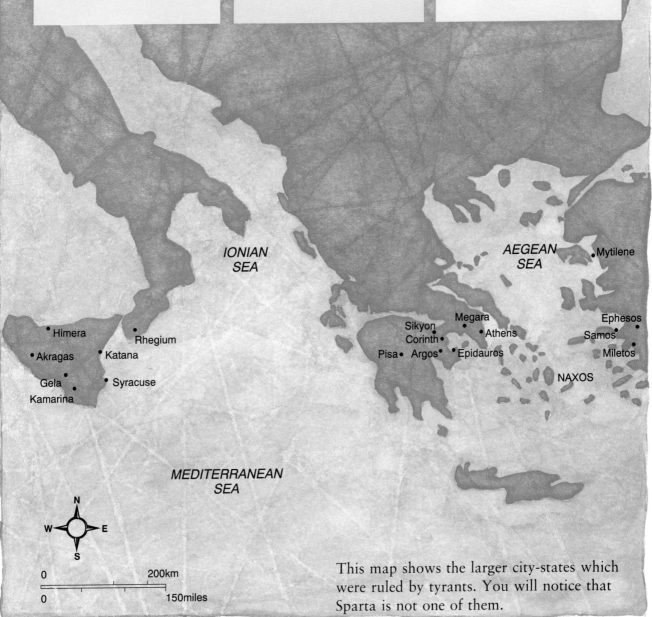

This map shows the larger city-states which were ruled by tyrants. You will notice that Sparta is not one of them.

Sparta

Spartans originally came from the north. They conquered the area of Laconia and became rulers there. Later, in the eighth century BC, they conquered Messenia and began to develop art, music, fine pottery and metalwork.

In 669 BC, the Spartans tried to conquer Argos, but they were defeated. Later in that century the people of Messenia, the Helots, rebelled against Spartan rule.

The Spartans were shocked by this and changed their ways. Legend tells of a great law-giver called Lycurgus who laid down rules for the state of Sparta to follow. Some of these rules are shown below.

Bronze statue of a Spartan soldier wearing his cloak and helmet

Officials decided whether a weak new-born baby should live or be left outside to die.

A boy left home when he was five years old to be trained by the state until he was twenty.

Boys were not expected to show any sign of weakness. There were thrashing competitions to see who could take the most pain without crying out. Some boys were beaten to death because they would not shout out.

A soldier joined the army when he was twenty years old and lived in barracks. He could not live with a wife until he was thirty. Most men lived in barracks until they were old.

The Assembly

This was all Spartan men over the age of thirty. Proposals by the *Gerousia* were listened to by the Assembly, and the members shouted 'yes' or 'no'. The loudest shout decided what was to be done.

Government

Sparta had its own system of goverment very different from the other city-states. Rule was shared between two kings, the *Gerousia* and the Assembly.

The Gerousia

This was a council of the two kings and 28 aristocrats. It was in charge of laws and policy.

Two kings

These were the leaders in war and religion.

The city of Sparta

Modern Sparta has few of the fine remains found in other Greek cities. This is partly because it was a city without walls. The Spartans believed that no enemy would ever reach their city because they were good fighters and Sparta was surrounded by high mountains.

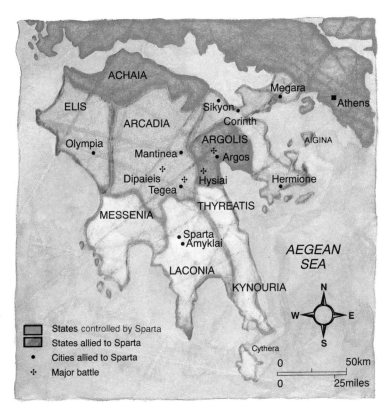

The Peloponnesian League

The Spartans realised that with only nine thousand male citizens they could not go on conquering other lands, because that would mean even more people to rule over and risk rebellion from. Instead they made agreements with other city-states in the area. Sparta became the leader of a group of city-states known as the Peloponnesian League.

The Helots

Spartan citizens were given land which was farmed for them by the Helots. The Helots were treated as serfs and had to give half of their crops to their Spartan master. The Helots were allowed to serve in the army. They rebelled from time to time.

Athens

For hundreds of years, Athens was the most powerful of all the city-states. Over 250 000 people lived in the city and surrounding area. It was a wealthy place where the arts flourished.

This is a replica of the huge gold and ivory statue of Athena that once stood inside the Parthenon.

Much of the Parthenon frieze showed young men on horseback.

Athena, the goddess of warfare and wisdom, was the patron of Athens. A temple dedicated to her was built on the highest point of the Acropolis (the upper fortified part of the city). This temple is called the Parthenon. Many thousands of tourists visit it each year.

The walls of the Parthenon were once decorated with a marble frieze showing a procession of worshippers during the festival of Great Panathenaic. This festival took place every four years. A new dress was woven for the statue of Athena and given to the priests.

In 1803, Lord Elgin removed some of the marble carvings. They can now be seen in the British Museum in London.

Power to the people

Athens did not have a king. It was probably
the first place to be ruled as a democracy,
although not everyone in Athens could vote.

The Assembly

The Assembly met forty times a year, usually at a hill called the Pnux.
All free male citizens over the age of eighteen could attend.
It decided on wars, officials, food supply and other important
matters. Some decisions could only be made if six thousand
citizens were present.

The Boule

This was a council of five hundred men aged
over thirty who gave advice to the Assembly.
Each person served for no more than
two years.

Could vote	Could not vote
male	female
over eighteen years old	poor people
	foreigners
Athenian parents	slaves

Strategoi

The ten tribes of Athens each
elected a military leader
called a *stategos*. The
ten *strategoi* could
be elected time
and time
again.

Slavery

Slaves made up about a quarter of the
working population of Athens. Most were
people who had been captured in warfare
and sold to slave dealers. They were then
put on sale in the slave market. Athenian
slaves were nearly all foreigners born north
or east of Athens in Asia Minor, Thrace or
the lands near the River Danube.

The Persian Wars

King Cyrus of the Persians expanded his empire westwards. In 546 BC, he took control of the Greek cities on the coast of Asia Minor. Sparta sent an envoy to warn Cyrus not to go any further. Cyrus asked, 'Who are the Spartans?'

In 499 BC, the Ionian cities revolted against Persian rule. They asked other Greek cities for help, but the revolt collapsed.

The Persians decided to attack the Greek cities in Europe. In 490 BC, the Battle of Marathon took place. The Athenians and their allies won a great victory.

The Athenians knew the Persians would be back. When silver was discovered in the area, they decided to spend the money on building a great fleet of ships.

In 480 BC, knowing the Persians planned to return, 31 Greek city-states agreed to fight together against the common enemy. The Spartans were chosen as leaders.

The Battle of Thermopylai

That same year, King Xerxes of Persia led his army of 150 000 men into Greece. The Greeks decided to make a stand at a mountain pass called Thermopylai where there were hot sulphur springs (*themopylai* means 'hot gates').

Xerxes heard that the Spartans were busy combing their long hair and doing gymnastics, and he laughed. But he stopped laughing when he was told that the Spartans comb their hair when they are ready to die.

Leonidas, the king of the Spartans, stood firm with the Greek soldiers. For two days the enemy made no impact. However, a Greek traitor told the Persians of a mountain track which their best soldiers (the Immortals) then followed in order to attack the Greeks from the rear.

Leonidas ordered most of the Greek army to retreat, but he stayed with three hundred Spartans and other allies. After a brave defence, he was killed along with all his soldiers.

In memory of Leonidas and the Spartans who died with him, the poet Simonides wrote these famous words:

'Stranger, go tell the Spartans that we lie here Obedient to their laws.'

The Battle of Salamis

As the Persian army approached Athens, women and children left the city. The men of Athens went to their ships ready to fight the Persian navy.

Themistocles, the Greek leader, tricked the Persians into an attack. He sent a trustworthy slave to them with a message. The slave pretended to be a traitor and told the Persians that if they attacked, the Greek fleet would sail away without fighting. Meanwhile the Greek fleet waited in the narrow channel between the mainland and the island of Salamis.

When the Persian ships advanced into the channel, they got in each other's way. The Greek ships were fitted with rams. They sailed into the Persian fleet and rammed the Persian ships into one another. Soon the sea was filled with wreckage and dead Persian bodies.

King Xerxes watched from his throne on the beach. The defeat at Salamis was so bad that he returned to Persia.

Home life

Men and women lived in different parts of the house. Women had the back or the upstairs part.

Wealthy Greek citizens owned slaves. This allowed both husbands and wives to be free of hard work, although the wife's main job was to supervise the slaves.

Poor Greeks might afford one slave, but many had none. Poor women worked alongside their husbands in town or country. They also looked after the children, collected the water and did the shopping. Rich women rarely went out.

This picture shows the home of a wealthy family

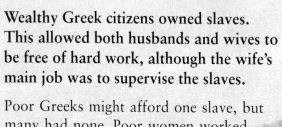

If a man brought male friends home for a meal, he was not joined by his wife or children.

Most people lived on vegetables, except at festival times when meat was eaten.

Each house had an altar where prayers were said every day. Wine was poured on the altar in honour of the gods.

Houses were built of brick. Few have survived so we cannot be sure how they were built.

Homes were cramped and not very clean.

There was little furniture.

Walls were not decorated.

Water had to be collected from a well. Some homes had a well in the courtyard.

Clothing was colourful.

How were the rooms heated?

How were the rooms lit at night?

Describe what the people in the picture are doing.

Describe the difference between a slave's room and a room where the owners lived.

Women in the city-states

Women led different lives in each of the city-states. Women citizens of Sparta led very different lives from those of Athens.

A terracotta pot shows a wedding procession with the bridegroom driving the bride to his family's hom

Athens

It did not matter whether a woman was rich or poor, free or a slave, she was still under the control of men. Women were not allowed to own property or deal in important business. They belonged to their father or guardian until they married. Then they became the property of their husband. The Greek writer Euripides wrote the following in a play called *Medea* in the fifth century BC:

'Of all living, thinking beings, we women are the most unlucky. First of all we have a dowry which must buy a husband to control us; not having a husband is worse. Secondly, there is the important question: is he a good husband? Women have no easy way out of marriage and cannot say no to their husbands.'

When a woman married, she brought a dowry (money or goods) to her husband. If her husband died, the dowry passed to whichever man then became her guardian.

Sparta

Unlike any other area of Greece, girls from Sparta were expected to exercise just like boys. It was thought that being healthy would make them strong mothers with healthy babies. Other Greeks made fun of Spartan women. Aristophanes wrote the following in a play called *Lysistrata* in the fifth century BC:

LYSISTRATA.   Greetings, dear Lampito. How is life in Sparta? What a colourful complexion! What strength! I reckon you could strangle a bull!

LAMPITO.   You could do the same, you know, with proper training. I have a thorough work-out every day.

Girl athlete from Sparta taking part in a race

Women in Sparta could own property, and up to 40 per cent of all land belonged to women. Work that was regarded as 'normal' for women in the rest of Greece – spinning and weaving – was done by slaves. Spartan women were trained to be wives and mothers of soldiers.

Views of women

The role of women differed depending on where they lived, their position in society and the period of history. It is also important to remember that most of what we read about women in Ancient Greece was written by men.

The frescoes from Knossos show that women in Minoan times had more freedom than in later times. Women are shown watching the games, mixing freely with men. In some scenes they can be seen taking part in bull-leaping.

Women of the Minoan Royal Court from a fresco at Knossos

'It was a custom in Crete that women also should be admitted to the games.'

Plutarch (first century AD)

The Greek writer Hesiod had a very low opinion of women. He wrote the following in the seventh century BC:

'Don't let any woman dazzle you . . . she's after your barn; anyone who trusts a woman is trusting thieves.'

Some women writers were popular. The most famous was Sappho. She was born about 630 BC on the island of Lesbos. Her poetry is mainly about love.

'Some say cavalry and others claim infantry or a fleet of long oars is the supreme sight on earth. I say it is the one you love.'

Sappho (seventh century BC)

A nineteenth-century artist's impression of Sappho

Wealthy women in Ancient Greece were expected to know how to spin, weave and cook. It was their job to make sure the slaves did their work properly. The Greek writer Xenophon wrote the following in a play called *Oeconomicus* in the fourth century BC:

Baking was a woman's job.

'**A husband should be pleased if he marries a wife who knows how to make woollen clothes, and how to share the work among female slaves.**'

Some female slaves worked as singers, dancers and musicians, entertaining at men-only parties.

Women were not taught to read or write. A few did become scholars, but it was not easy. Some dressed as men in order to be educated alongside them.

'**The ability to think is not present in slaves. It does not work in women. It is not yet developed in children . . . The male is by nature superior and the female inferior and the one rules and the other is ruled.**'

The Greek philosopher Aristotle (fourth century BC)

There is little evidence to tell us what women thought of the way they were treated. Sappho created a world in her poetry where women were equal to men. She described women as 'complete human beings'.

Vase showing a slave playing the double-pipes to male guests at a drinking party

Education for life

Only Sparta provided free education. People in other city-states had to pay, so the poor probably received little education. Different teachers were employed to teach different subjects. Most were badly paid.

One teacher taught reading and writing. Pupils practised using a wax tablet. If the pupil was not making progress, the teacher could beat him.

Boys

Most boys from wealthy families were educated. Physical education was part of the preparation that all male citizens needed for their time in the army.

A music teacher taught the lyre. Educated Greeks were expected to play an instrument and to be able to sing in a choir.

A sports teacher taught running, jumping, javelin, discus, boxing and wrestling.

The hoplites

The Spartans had a permanent army, but other city-states depended on citizens fighting whenever there was a need. Greek armies in the fifth century BC depended mainly on hoplites. These were citizens who could afford to equip themselves with a round shield, long spear, short sword, breast-plate, helmet and leg guards. Some hoplites had a slave to carry their equipment.

Poorer citizens could not afford this type of equipment. They served as light-armed soldiers and threw stones and javelins at the enemy.

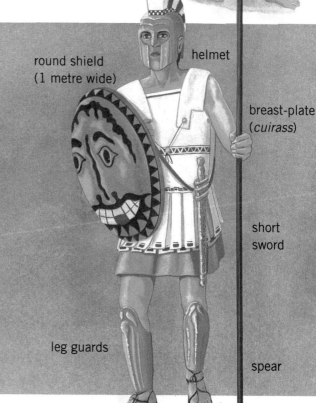

round shield (1 metre wide)

helmet

breast-plate (*cuirass*)

short sword

leg guards

spear

Girls

Very few girls were sent to teachers for an education. Instead their mothers taught them how to do household jobs.

weaving

cooking

looking after children

cleaning

combing wool

spinning wool

A girl could have her marriage arranged when she was only five years old. She would probably marry at the age of fourteen. Her husband would be much older than her, often over thirty. The Ancient Greeks did not believe that love was necessary for marriage.

Medicine: science or religion?

The writers of history books often praise the Ancient Greeks for their skills in medicine. They use the evidence available to them at the time of writing.

There is evidence about Ancient Greek medicine in the writings of Homer. In the *Iliad*, Homer describes how Menelaos was hit by an arrow which stayed in his body. A doctor named Machaon was sent for:

> 'At once he pulled the arrow out, and as it was pulled the sharp barbs broke backwards. When he saw the wound where the bitter arrow had entered, he sucked out the blood and skilfully placed healing medicines on it.'

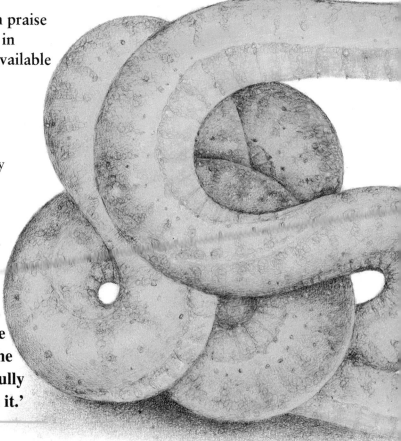

Fourth-century BC carving of Asklepios treating a patient

In Greek legend, Machaon was the son of Asklepios.

Asklepios was probably a successful doctor who lived around 1200 BC. After his death, legends about his skills spread far and wide. Asklepios was later worshipped as the god of healing. Temples known as *asklepaeia* were built to him. Sick people travelled to them and prayed to the god to be cured.

Patients stayed at the temples and were given rest and special diets. They were then moved into a special room called the *abaton*. Here it seems they were given a drug. In their sleep they dreamt of a visit by the god Asklepios and his daughters, Hygeia and Panacea. Large snakes would lick the patient's wounds.

Hippocrates

Hippocrates is a famous Greek doctor who did not accept that the gods caused and cured illness. He was born on the island of Kos around 460 BC.

This kind of thinking changed the way doctors worked. Many of Hippocrates' ideas are still shared by doctors today. He believed patients should be carefully examined before any treatment began. He and others wrote books about medicine which doctors could learn from.

> **'If we can find the cause, we can cure the disease.'**
>
> *Hippocrates (fifth century BC)*

Joseph Carter and his team of archaeologists have excavated over 350 graves at Metaponto.

New evidence

Since 1974 the archaeologist Joseph Carter has been excavating the Ancient Greek colony at Metaponto in southern Italy. His team has found that:

- many children died young

- adults lived on average to the age of forty

- many people suffered from malaria

- most broken bones were never set by doctors.

One citizen had written in his tomb the names of fifteen doctors on whom he had placed a curse.

Religion

The Ancient Greeks believed the gods were rather like people in the way they behaved. They argued, fought, had love affairs, lied and helped others.

The power of the gods was immense. They could change the events of history by helping one person against another. Some fell in love with human beings. Zeus had many love affairs with mortal women. His wife, the goddess Hera, would become angry because of this and punish the women and their children!

Use reference books to find out:

- the role of each god
- a myth told about a god.

Oracles

The Ancient Greeks believed it was possible to foretell the future. They would visit an oracle who could communicate with the gods.

The greatest oracle was at Delphi, where the god Apollo could be questioned about the future. Poor people paid less than rich people to consult her. However, she often gave an answer that had two meanings.

One day the wealthy King Croesus visited her:

Should I fight the Persians?

If you do, a great empire will fall.

King Croesus fought the Persians, but the empire which fell was his own.

Vase-painting of the oracle at Delphi inhaling volcanic fumes to put herself into a trance

The journey of the dead

When someone in Ancient Greece died, the relatives followed a set ritual.

Relatives wore black. An *obolos* (small coin) was placed in the mouth of the corpse.

The body was carried to the cemetery. Mourners would weep and wail loudly.

Bodies could be buried or cremated. Personal objects were buried with them.

The Ancient Greeks believed the soul entered Hades, the underworld, after death. Hades was a marshy land surrounded by water. The first task of the dead person's soul was to cross the water.

The *obolos* was given to Charon, the ferryman. No coin, no crossing: the soul was doomed to wander the water's edge for ever! At the far side, the soul was judged and sent to one of three places.

The **good** went to the Elysian Fields. These were meadows full of flowers where the soul lived a slow, pleasurable life.

The **ordinary** were sent to the Asphodel Fields, which were shady and boring. Things could be improved if the relatives who were still alive made sacrifices and prayed for the dead soul.

The **bad** had a terrible time in Tartarus. They received punishment for ever.

The arts

The arts played an important part in Greek life. Magnificent pottery can still be seen today in many of the world's museums. Music, dance, mosaics, jewellery and painting were also important in Ancient Greece.

Statues

Statues provide some of the finest examples of Greek art still seen today. The style, however, changed over time. Compare the two statues on this page. The first is from the seventh century BC.
It shows a young man whose face has no expression and whose body is based on a standard idea rather than on direct observation. The second is from the third century BC. It shows a dying Celt. Notice the detail of his ribs and the blood running from his wounds.

The ancient theatre at Epidauros

Theatre

Most parts of the Greek world had large open-air theatres which seated thousands of spectators.

The central area held the chorus. This was a group of men who told the story to the audience. The actors performed on a raised stage behind the chorus.

All parts were played by men. The actors wore masks. To change characters they simply changed masks.

Philip and Alexander

War raged throughout the Greek lands in the first half of the fourth century BC. Athens, Sparta, Thebes and the princes of the Persian Empire battled for control of the city-states and islands. However, it was not from any of these famous cities that the future leader of the Greeks came. Instead it was a king from the north, an area regarded as backwards by most of the Ancient Greeks.

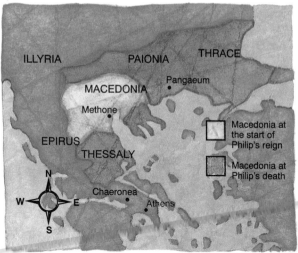

Philip's empire

Philip of Macedon

In 359 BC, Philip II became leader of a small, poor city state called Macedonia. He trained his army and began to conquer other Greek states. When those to the south opposed him, he defeated them in a battle at Chaeronea in 338 BC. He was about to lead all the Greek states in a war against Persia when he was assassinated.

Most Greek city-states thought the Macedonians were old-fashioned. They did not like the idea of kings in power. Demosthenes, an Athenian statesman, called Philip a 'barbarian'.

Philip's achievements

- trained his army
- invented a new weapon: the five-metre-long pike (a type of spear)
- began to conquer other Greek states
- encouraged new farming methods
- increased trade
- built new towns
- minted coins of a high quality

Soldiers at the rear of Philip's army held their pikes upright.

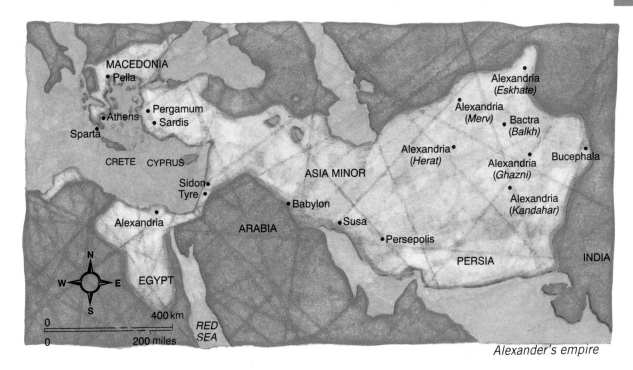

Alexander's empire

Alexander the Great

Philip's son Alexander was only twenty years old when he became King of Macedonia. He was famous as a great warrior even then.

Alexander wanted to create an empire where the Greek language was widely spoken, where a single Greek currency was used, and where cities were built to reflect Greek culture. He did not want the people of his empire to be slaves.

Alexander invaded Asia Minor in 334 BC. In the next eleven years he won victory after victory, reaching as far as India.

Alexander treated European and Asian people as equals. He and his commanders married aristocratic Asian women. He also had a multiracial army.

Alexander died of fever in Babylon in the year 323 BC.

Alexander's sarcophagus shows him in battle.

Alexander's new towns

- Alexander built seventy new towns.
- Each town had 10 000 men from different races.
- The city of Alexandria in Egypt still bears his name today.

Greeks and Romans

After Alexander's death, his empire quickly broke up into many kingdoms. But the influence of Greek culture continued. The period after his death is known as the Hellenic Age (the Greeks called themselves Hellenes). It was a time when Greek ideas and the Greek way of life spread far and wide.

Meanwhile a new empire was already growing based on the city of Rome. As the Romans gained control of most of Italy, they came more and more into contact with the Greek cities on the coast of southern Italy. These pictures show how Greek ideas influenced the Romans:

Rome later conquered large parts of what had been Alexander's empire. The last of the Macedonian rulers was Cleopatra of Egypt, who was defeated by Rome in 30 BC. (You can read more about this period in the BBC Fact Finder on Egypt.)

coinage

theatre

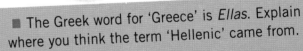

learning

gods

sculpture

■ The Greek word for 'Greece' is *Ellas*. Explain where you think the term 'Hellenic' came from.

■ Find out more about some of the Greek influences on the Romans. Why do you think their influences were so strong?

■ Look at the photograph of Kuretes Street in the city of Ephesus (page 45).

What is the road made of?

What do you think lined each side of the road? Give a reason for your answer.

■ The two-storey building at the bottom of the street was the library. What does this tell us about the Hellenic Age?

Ephesus

Many Greek cities became centres of Roman rule. The city of Ephesus was founded by the Greeks from across the Aegean Sea. It became one of the five main cities of the Roman Empire.

Visitors today are amazed at the remains of this Hellenic–Roman city. They can walk along Kuretes Street (below) towards the Library of Celsius in much the same way as Emperor Hadrian once did.

Interpretations of the past

The work of archaeologists and historians helps us to understand life in Ancient Greece. Even so, we cannot be sure about the past. We can only say what we *think* happened, based on the evidence available to us.

The story of Theseus and the Minotaur (see pages 8–9) has been told and enjoyed for thousands of years.

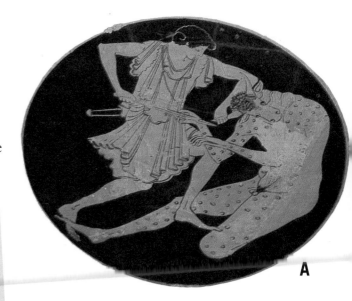

A

Describe what pictures **A** and **B** show.

List the similarities and differences between the two pictures.

One of the pictures has been taken from a wine cup dating from the sixth century BC. The other is by the famous twentieth-century artist Picasso. Say which is which and give reasons why you think the artists painted them in these ways.

B

C

D

Pictures **C** and **D** both show Theseus on his return to Athens.

■ Compare pictures C and D with what you have learned in this book about Ancient Greece. Think about:

architecture

clothes and fashion

musical instruments

materials

the role of women

■ Picture C was painted by Rene of Anjou in the fifteenth century AD. Find other paintings from that time and list the similarities with Picture C.

Index

Photo credits
Allsport pp. 4 (left), 5 B. Martin; Ancient Art and Architecture Collection pp. 16, 36, 43; Antikenmuseum, Staatliche Museen Preußischer Kulturbesitz, Berlin/Ingrid Geske p. 38; Berggruen Collection on loan to the National Gallery, London p. 46 (bottom) *Minotauromachy 1935, Pablo Picasso* © DACS 1994; Peter Clayton pp. 17 (right), 46 (top); C. M. Dixon pp. 33 (top), 40 (right); Robert Harding Picture Library pp. 14, 45; Museum of Herakleion, Greece p. 32 (top); Michael Holford pp. 15, 17 (left), 24 (right), 31, 41; Institute of Classical Archaeology, University of Texas p. 37; Nikos Kontos, Athens pp. 12–13; The Mansell Collection pp. 18, 32 (bottom); The Metropolitan Museum of Art pp. 30 *Purchase Walter C. Baker Gift, 1956 (56.11.1)* Rollout photograph by J. Kerr, 40 (left) *Fletcher Fund, 1932 (32.11.1)*, 47 (bottom) *Purchase, Joseph Pulitzer Bequest, 1953 (53.11.4)*; Österreichische Nationalbibliothek p. 47 (top) *E1622-C. Cod.2617, f. 39*; Rex Features p. 4 (right) N Jorgensen; Royal Ontario Museum, Toronto, Canada p. 24 (left); Spectrum Colour Library pp. 10, 11 I. Meredith; Staatliche Antikensammlungen und Glyptothek München/Studio Koppermann p. 33 (bottom); Wadsworth Atheneum, Hartford. Gift of J. Pierpont Morgan p. 22
Front cover: C. M. Dixon: Gold death mask of an Achaean king ('Agamemnon') from Mycenae

Illustrations
© Wayne Anderson 1993 **pages 8–9, 36–37, 38–39**; © David Ashby 1993 **pages 14–15**; © Philip Hood 1993 **pages 2–3, 16, 17, 19, 20, 24–25, 28–29**; © Brent Linley 1993 **pages 4, 5, 6–7, 10, 21, 23, 42 (top), 43**; © Shirley Mallinson 1993 **pages 18, 22, 26–27, 30, 34, 35, 41, 42 (bottom), 44**

Published by BBC Educational Publishing,
Woodlands, 80 Wood Lane,
London W12 0TT

First published 1993
Reprinted 1996, 1997

© Steve and Patricia Harrison/BBC Education 1993
The moral rights of the authors have been asserted.

Paperback ISBN 0 563 35385 6
Hardback ISBN 0 563 35386 4

Printed and bound in Great Britain by
Cambus Litho Ltd, East Kilbride